Marilyn Monroe

A Brief Biography from Beginning to the End

The Biography

History Hub

No part of this publication may be reproduced or retransmitted, electronic or mechanical, without the written permission of the publisher. First Published in the USA.

Copyright © 2020 by *History Hub*. All Rights Reserved.

Terms of Use: Product names, logos, brands, and other trademarks featured or referred to within this publication are the property of their respective trademark holders and are not affiliated with this publication. The information in this book is meant for educational purposes only, and the publisher and author make no representations or warranties with respect to the accuracy or completeness of these contents and disclaim all warranties such as warranties of fitness for a particular purpose.

Participant of: www.kindlepromos.com Free Kindle Library

CONTENTS

Part One: Editor Foreword

Chapter One: A Life from Beginning to End

Chapter Two: Adolescence, Teenage & Adult Years

Chapter Three: Career and family life

Chapter Four: The Person Behind the Fame

Chapter Five: Conclusion (includes legacy, their works affected us today)

Your Free Bonus Download

Part One: Editor Foreword

"Those who don't know history are doomed to repeat it." — Edmund Burke

More than ever, it is important that we equip ourselves with the power of knowledge to learn from the lessons of mistakes from the past to ensure that we do not fall victim to similar mistakes. It is our aim to provide quality history books for readers to learn important history lessons critical for everyone. And we'd like to make sure you learn the stories faster, and more efficiently.

This is why we are constantly updating our catalog with new releases in History Hub. You can access the catalog of all the new titles here. Thanks for reading, History Hub

Attention: Get Your Free Gift Now

Every purchase now comes with a FREE Bonus Gift

2020 Top 5 Fireside Books of the Year
(New-York Times Bestsellers, USA Today & more)

Chapter One: A Life from Beginning to End

Birth and Early Childhood

Did You Know?

Marilyn Monroe was nine when she went to the orphanage. She had no choice because her mother was committed to a mental institution after being diagnosed with paranoid schizophrenia.

†††

She was born Norma Jeane in Los Angeles, California, on June 1, 1926. Tragically, she ended up in an orphanage when her mother was diagnosed with paranoid schizophrenia. The young Norma Jeanne would suffer abuses at the hand of various foster care, forcing her back to the orphanage. When her mother's best friend finally became her legal guardian, Norma Jeane came to live with her.

At 16, Norma Jeane got married to avoid going back to the orphanage. In Sta. Catalina, Norma Jeane became a bored housewife. However, she would soon taste her first success with modeling. Norma Jeane became the most popular pin-up girl in history. Not long, Norma Jeanne faced a choice between her marriage and a career in Hollywood. She ended up signing a contract with Fox, filing for a divorce, and changing her name to Marilyn Monroe.

At the start of her Hollywood career, Marilyn Monroe would appear in several minor film roles. Her success was not instantaneous. Like many other young actresses, Monroe had to hustle behind the scenes. She took different lessons, learning how to act, sing, and dance. She socialized with sleazy Hollywood executives to catch her break in showbusiness, enduring the dreaded Hollywood casting couch. Monroe would sign new short contracts with Fox executives, including some immoral dealings behind closed doors. It was standard practice in the male-dominated showbiz during that time.

When she met talent agent Johnny Hyde, Monroe felt blessed. He would single-handedly save her from the Hollywood predators. Hyde helped negotiate a new seven-year deal with Fox, landing her better roles in future movies. He taught Monroe how to use the press to her advantage. Learning from her new friend, she would talk to the media candidly to gain public support. Monroe received thousands of letters from fans, and critics started praising her acting. The showbiz news predicted that she would become a future star. Her popularity was on the rise. Sadly, Johnny Hyde would die suddenly from a heart attack, leaving Monroe devastated.

By 1953, Marilyn Monroe had achieved true Hollywood fame. She was Fox's biggest star. Unfortunately, Fox made tons of money, but Monroe remained underpaid. They forced her to play the dumb blonde bombshell, but she refused. This ultimately led to her suspension, but during this break, Marilyn found love.

In 1954, she married baseball star Joe DiMaggio. Meanwhile, Fox gave her a new contract, granting her more money and more creative control over her roles and public image. Things were looking up again. Her next film, The Seven Year Itch (1955), became the year's biggest movie. However, her husband went berserk. He hated her sexy image in Hollywood and wanted her to stop. She, in turn, found him too controlling. Their marriage was over after nine months. After the divorce, DiMaggio would stalk her as he was still in love.

Monroe's reputation inside Hollywood was getting worse. She would show up on the set late or didn't even show up at all. Monroe forgot lines and would rely too much on her acting coach, infuriating her co-stars and directors. Everybody now believed it would always be tough to work with Marilyn Monroe.

By 1956, Monroe married a third time to playwright Arthur Miller, but her third time was not the charm. After a few months in the marriage, he realized he hated her. Miller found her embarrassing for his status. He became cold and cruel towards her. Monroe tried to make the marriage work. She got pregnant three times but lost all of them due to complications. Feeling devastated, she attempted suicide several times, all unsuccessful. Her third marriage lasted four and a half years.

Her bad reputation in Hollywood continued to grow. Everybody hated working with her, but Monroe continued to find work because her movies make huge money. She had an established fanbase. The public loved her, and female fans adored her.

In 1962, Monroe made her last film. Problems plagued the unfinished movie right from the start. Monroe needed time to rest because she was too sick to work. However, Fox didn't care. They demanded the shooting to start on schedule. Fox even fired Monroe when she went on sick leave. They eventually renegotiated and convinced Monroe to come back. She agreed, but Monroe would never return for work.

On August 5, 1962, her maid asked for help when Monroe failed to respond to her knocks. Dr. Ralph Greenson came and broke a window to enter her bedroom. They found her lifeless body, lying naked and facing down. She had one hand on the phone receiver, and beside her was an empty bottle of Nembutal, her sleeping pills. Toxicology showed that she died from an overdose of barbiturates.

Fireside Question 1

††ature†

Norma Jeane's mother was diagnosed with paranoid schizophrenia. Do you believe that Marilyn Monroe inherited her depression from her mother?

Fireside Question 2

†††

Norma Jeane suffered from abuse from foster care. Do you think this affected Marilyn Monroe's emotional state during her Hollywood career?

Fireside Question 3

†††

Marilyn Monroe endured the Hollywood casting couch. Did this cause her depression?

Fireside Question 4

†††

Talent agent Jonathan Hyde helped Monroe in her career. Do you believe there are still some good men in Hollywood today? Or are they all like Harvey Weinstein?

Fireside Question 5

†††

Marilyn Monroe was found dead inside her bedroom with both doors and windows locked from the inside. Do you believe in the conspiracy that her death was not a suicide?

Chapter Two: Adolescence, Teenage, and Adult Years

Did You Know?

Marilyn Monroe got married when she was only sixteen. She stayed with Grace Goddard, her mother's best friend. When Grace and her husband needed to move to West Virginia, she couldn't bring Marilyn with them unless she got married. So, Marilyn married her next-door neighbor to avoid going back to the orphanage.

†††

In 1921, Marilyn's mother, Gladys Pearl Baker, divorced Jasper Newton Baker, her husband of four years, because of marital abuse. After losing custody over their kids, Jackie and Berniece, Jasper kidnapped and raised them in his hometown in Kentucky. However, Gladys didn't go after them because it would cost her more money to take care of her kids by herself.

By 1924, Gladys married Martin Edward Mortenson, but they would soon separate when she met Charles Stanley Gifford at RKO Pictures. While working as a film cutter, she got pregnant with Charles' baby. Gladys soon after applied for her second divorce.

On June 1, 1926, Norma Jeane was born. Gladys used Mortenson's last name on the birth certificate. In contrast, the grandmother, Della Mae Monroe Hogan, used Baker on the baptismal certificate to hide the illegitimacy. Norma Jeane would find out about Gifford later in her life, but he didn't want anything to do with her, stating he was happily married.

An Evangelical Christian couple living in the rural town of Hawthorne, Albert and Ida Bolender, came to the picture to help. They acted as foster parents to a two-weeks old Norma Jeane. While Gladys continued to work in the city, she would visit her daughter during the weekends. Norma Jeane was happy growing up with the Bolender family, but that was soon going to change.

In 1933, Gladys bought a small house in Hollywood and took Norma Jeane to stay with her. They rented their extra spaces to actors and their families. Everything was going great until news of Jackie Baker's death came along. Gladys was so devastated that she even told her seven-year-old daughter that it should have been her who died and not her son. Gladys had suffered a complete mental breakdown. Diagnosed with paranoid schizophrenia, she would spend a lot of time in and out of psychiatric care for the rest of her life, with almost little to no contact with her daughter.

Norma Jeane had become a ward of the state and would struggle to live a normal childhood. She would spend most of her time bouncing from the orphanage and eleven different foster homes. Norma Jeane got molested on several occasions during foster care. The only happy moments she had during those trying times were when her foster family would send her to the movies. Norma Jeane recalled staying all day and way into the night in front of the big screen, all alone in the theatre. She didn't care because she loved it there. It was her sanctuary. Norma Jeane found joy and wished someday she would become an actress and become a movie star.

When Norma Jeane was back at the Los Angeles orphanage, she felt abandoned and unwanted. Norma Jeane was a shy girl and became more withdrawn from her suffering. She even developed a stutter because of the abuse. Clara Grace Goddard, Gladys best friend, took pity on the neglected girl. So, when she became the legal guardian of Norma Jean in 1936, she removed the young girl from the orphanage to live with her and her new husband, Erwin Doc Goddard. However, when her husband also abused Norma Jeane, Grace sent the poor girl to live with Ana Atchinson Lower, her aunt. Norma Jeane would stay there for five years.

In September 1938, she enrolled at Ralph Waldo Emerson Community Charter Middle School. Although regarded as an average student, Norma Jeane did excel in writing. She composed many articles for her school's newspaper. When Ana Lower's health deteriorated, Norma Jeane returned to live with the Goddards in 1941. She enrolled at Van Nuys High School.

In 1942, the Goddards needed to move to West Virginia and couldn't take Norma Jeane with them. Unless she got married, she must go back to the orphanage. So, Norma Jeane waited until she turned 16 to marry her 21-year-old neighbor, James Dougherty. She dropped out of school to become a housewife. The following year, the young couple moved to Santa Catalina Island.

Fireside Question 6

†††

When her husband kidnapped her two kids to Kentucky, Gladys didn't go after them because it would cost her more money to take care of her kids by herself. If you were in her shoes, would you also do the same, or would you go after the kids?

Fireside Question 7

†††

Norma Jeane was fine, growing up with the Bolenders. When Gladys had a mental breakdown, why was Norma Jeane not sent back to the Bolenders? Do you believe she would be better with them than go to the orphanage?

Fireside Question 8

†††

Norma Jeane suffered abuse during foster care, causing her to go back to the orphanage. Why were the abusers not punished? Was there no law to protect children from predators during those times?

Fireside Question 9

†††

When Grace Goddard found out her husband molested Norma Jeane, she sent the poor girl to live with her aunt. How could she turn a blind eye to the abuse? Why didn't she divorce her husband and give proper care to Norma Jeane?

Fireside Question 10

†††

Instead of going back to the orphanage, Norma Jeane decided to get married at 16. Was that the right thing to do? Would you also do that if you were in her shoes?

Chapter Three: Career and Family Life

Did You Know?

Frank Sinatra gave Marilyn Monroe a dog as a gift. The Maltese Terrier was named Mafia Honey, Maf for short. When Monroe passed away, Sinatra's secretary Gloria Lovell took Maf in.

†††

Photographer David Conover discovered Norma Jeane. A bored housewife working in a factory, destiny called her to become a model. And that's what she did.

Bleaching her hair blonde, Norma Jeane appeared in swimsuits in various Men's magazines. Under the pseudonym Jean Norman, she became the most popular girl in pin-up history.

In 1946, 20th Century Fox came and offered her a contract under the condition that she became non-marital. Norma Jean chose Fox, and her first marriage was now over.

Ben Lyon of Fox took one look at Norma Jean and said that she reminded him of Broadway star Marilyn Miller. Norma Jeane suggested Monroe from her grandmother, and they agreed to the name. And so, Marilyn Monroe was born.

Marilyn took acting lessons while appearing in a series of minor film roles. Behind the scenes, Monroe had to mingle with top producers and directors. She even endured the so-called Hollywood casting couch just to get movie roles.

Monroe continued to model, appearing in a beer commercial and posing nude for calendars. She was growing out of her shyness as she became more confident and had no problem with nudity. Monroe would later pose for Playboy, even at the height of her career.

Not long, Monroe met talent agent Johnny Hyde. Saving her from the Hollywood predators, he helped her land more supporting roles in movies without having to grant anyone special favors. Hyde successfully negotiated a seven-year deal with Fox for her.

Her popularity was now on the rise as she received thousands of letters from fans. Critics also noticed her, praising her as a possible future star. When Hyde suddenly died of a heart attack, Monroe was heartbroken. She lost the only man who was not taking advantage of her in the business. She attempted suicide by overdose but was luckily saved by her acting coach.

Her private life was a mess. To further her career, Monroe was in short relationships with various directors and actors. She even capitalized on her nude scandal, admitting that she was broke at that time. Monroe quickly gained public sympathy, and Fox took full advantage of it. They used Monroe's sex appeal, offering her leading roles.

1953 cemented Marilyn Monroe as a true Hollywood star. Her femme fatale role in Niagara secured her place as a sex symbol, while Gentlemen Prefer Blondes and How to Marry a Millionaire established her dumb blonde persona. All three films made tons of money for Fox, making Marilyn Monroe their biggest star. However, she was not getting paid much compared to the other actresses. Disappointed by getting typecast and underpaid, Monroe refused her next film project, which led to her suspension.

Not long after, Monroe was on the front pages again. She was in love, falling for baseball star Joe DiMaggio. They got married in 1954. Fox realized their mistake and signed Monroe to a new contract, giving her more creative control and a higher salary. The Seven Year Itch (1955) would become the highest box office success of her career. However, Joe DiMaggio hated Monroe's sexy image. He went berserk and beat Marilyn after filming the infamous subway grate scene. Their marriage ended shortly, lasting only nine months.

Marilyn had a reputation of being difficult to work as she would have a habit of arriving on-set late. Sometimes, she didn't even bother showing up at all. Monroe would forget lines, requiring several takes. She was over-dependent on her acting coaches, infuriating co-stars and directors. Unbeknownst to them, Monroe was in constant pain from endometriosis. She also found herself with low self-esteem from the persistent sexism and objectification by her directors and co-stars.

Monroe married playwright Arthur Miller in 1956, surprising everybody. The nerd gets to marry the prom queen, as they say. However, her third marriage was a mistake. Monroe got pregnant three times but losing all of them to miscarriage. Miller regretted marrying her, finding her embarrassing. He wrote all his disappointments in his journal and purposely left it for Monroe to read. She was heartbroken that their marriage was over.

Her bad reputation suffered further on the set of Some Like It Hot (1959). Her co-star Tony Curtis stated that he would rather kiss Hitler than work with her. Nevertheless, the film was a massive hit and earned Monroe her first win at the Golden Globe for Best Actress.

Nothing changed for her on the set of Misfits (1961). Everybody hated working with her, except for one co-star, Clark Gable. When he passed away after filming ended, Monroe cried for days.

Something's Got To Give (1962) would be her last film. The unfinished movie was full of disaster right from the start. Monroe fell too sick to work and needed time off, but Fox demanded the filming to continue on schedule. When she went on sick leave, they fired her, replacing her with Lee Remick. When co-star Dean Martin refused to work with anybody but Monroe, Fox sued him as well and shut everything down. Fox would later back down and renegotiate with Monroe. Shooting would start again soon. However, on August 5, 1962, Marilyn Monroe died from an overdose of barbiturates.

Fireside Question 11

†††

20th Century Fox made Norma Jeane choose between them and her marriage. She went for a Hollywood career over her husband. What would you pick if you were in that situation?

Fireside Question 12

†††

Norma Jean and Ben Lyon came up with the stage name Marilyn Monroe. Do you think she succeeded because of her stage name? Or do you believe she would triumph with any other name?

Fireside Question 13

†††

Despite having a contract, Marilyn Monroe needed to endure the dreaded Hollywood casting couch to further her career. What would you do if you were in her shoes? Would you tolerate the sexism?

Fireside Question 14

†††

Monroe created her sex symbol image to the public, using it to her full advantage. The press and the fans loved her for that. Do you agree with her tactic? What other strategy can she use to succeed further?

Fireside Question 15

†††

Fox was making tons of money from all of Marilyn Monroe's films. Why would they refuse to give her a better contract? Why would they continue to short-change Monroe by making her underpaid?

Chapter Four: the Person Behind the Fame

Main Difficulties to Overcome in Life

Did You Know?

Marilyn Monroe loved books. She carried a book with her most of the time. Monroe was well-read and such a bookworm that she owned over 400 books when she passed away.

†††

Her difficulties started even before she was born. Her mother Gladys conceived Norma Jeane illegitimately. Her father was never in the picture throughout her life.

Norma Jeane would never enjoy a normal childhood. She spent her youth bouncing from the orphanage and eleven foster homes. After getting molested several times in foster care, Norma Jeane would return to the orphanage. She developed a stutter and had become withdrawn. When Norma Jeane came to live with her legal guardian, her step-father abused her too. She had to overcome these traumas. Norma Jeane went on to live with her aging aunt for five years. She would return to her guardian when her aunt's health deteriorated.

In school, she was an average student but showed excellence in writing. Norma Jeane contributed to her school's newspaper. She also loved to read, which helped her to become a better writer. When Norma Jeane married her neighbor at the age of 16, she stopped attending school.

Her first achievement came as a model. Using the pseudonym Jean Norman, she modeled for magazine covers and advertisements. She soon became the most popular girl in pin-up history.

Her next difficulty came with Fox Studio. They made her pick between her marriage and a film career – she chose to become Marilyn Monroe.

Early on in Hollywood, she had to hustle. While attending acting lessons, Monroe also mingled with the predators of Hollywood. She endured the infamous casting couch and serviced executives to get roles in movies. Sadly, it was all part of her dubious contractual agreement with Fox.

When talent agent Johnny Hyde came into her life, Monroe was ecstatic. She felt blessed because he saved her from the sleazy Hollywood decision-makers. Hyde helped her land better roles and negotiated a seven-year deal with Fox. Monroe owed her break to her new friend. Sadly, he died shortly after, leaving her heartbroken. Monroe attempted suicide because she lost the one man who was helping her career. Fortunately, her acting coach found and saved her.

Monroe was determined to succeed, doing everything she can to further her career. These included plastic surgery and dating several different actors and directors. Monroe learned to use the press to her advantage. Not long, the media and the public would love her, especially the women and soldiers. Calling her the IT GIRL, they were always on her side.

Monroe became so popular that she was Fox's biggest star. She continued to take acting lessons because Monroe wanted to become a better actress. It paid off as Monroe won her Golden Globe Best Actress for her role in Some Like It Hot (1959), proving to everybody that she was not only a sex symbol.

Throughout her Hollywood career, she had to overcome Fox. They were constantly taking advantage of her. She remained underpaid despite Fox earning loads of money from her movies. Typecasting her with sexy dumb blonde roles, Fox would suspend Monroe if she didn't comply. It continued up to her last film with them.

Meanwhile, Monroe found love two more times. She fell for baseball star Joe DiMaggio, but their marriage lasted only nine months. He was controlling and hated her sexy image in Hollywood. They divorced, and she would later marry playwright Arthur Miller. He ended up being cruel to her as well. She also lost three pregnancies with him, adding more emotional trauma to her already complicated life.

Everybody in Hollywood knew that it was tough to work with Monroe. She would either show up late on the set or not at all. Directors and co-stars hated working with her. Monroe would forget lines, requiring more takes. She became too dependent on her acting coaches, infuriating the sexist directors and male co-stars. Hollywood didn't care that she was suffering from incurable endometriosis. Monroe sadly became addicted to sleeping pills, painkillers, and alcohol.

In 1962, Monroe performed her iconic Happy Birthday, Mr. President for JFK. She wore a beaded skin-tight gown while singing in her sultry voice.

After her death, DiMaggio was heartbroken. He never remarried. DiMaggio regularly sent roses to her grave. And after 36 years, DiMaggio died, stating that he would finally get to meet Marilyn.

In 1999, Monroe was voted the sexiest woman of the century by People's Magazine. Playboy selected her as #1 Sex Star of the 20th Century. And the American Film Institute ranked her #6 on the AFI's 50 Greatest Screen Legends of the Golden Age of Hollywood.

Fireside Question 16

†††

Her mother suffered a mental illness while her father was never non-existent. Do you believe Marilyn Monroe would have avoided emotional troubles if she grew up in a happier family? Would she enjoy a normal childhood?

Fireside Question 17

†††

Marilyn Monroe was successful with her modeling career. Do you think she should have stuck to modeling instead of trying her luck in Hollywood?

Fireside Question 18

†††

Johnny Hyde helped Marilyn Monroe, but he died suddenly. Do you believe Marilyn Monroe would have become more successful if Hyde didn't die?

Fireside Question 19

†††

Marilyn Monroe married three times. Who do you think was her best husband, and why?

Fireside Question 20

†††

Marilyn Monroe was in constant pain. She was also suffering from depression. What are some of the causes of her pain and suffering?

Chapter Five: Conclusion (includes legacy, their works affected us today)

Did You Know?

Actor Warren Beatty was among the last few people to see Marilyn Monroe alive. The 25-year-old actor met Marilyn Monroe for the first time at a party. He recalled playing the piano when Monroe asked him to take a walk with her by the beach. Beatty could sense her deep sorrow during their time together. Monroe was dead the very next morning.

†††

Marilyn Monroe remained one of the most famous women in history. When she died in 1962, Monroe left her $1.6 million worth of estate to Lee Strasberg, her acting coach. He managed it, setting up trust funds for both Gladys and Berniece, her half-sister. When Lee died in 1982, his wife inherited the estate. She soon allowed the licensing of Marilyn Monroe, its name, image, and likeness. It increased the value of the Marilyn Monroe estate.

Her memorabilia can fetch a lot of money. Mariah Carey bought Monroe's baby Grand Piano for $662,500. In 2011, the estate got $5.6 million for the infamous white dress from The Seven Year Itch (1955). And billionaire Jimmy Pattison acquired the beaded Happy Birthday gown for $6.3 million.

Her millions of adoring fans worshiped her, loving her sexy blonde bombshell persona. Marilyn Monroe has influenced new generations of women, including several celebrities and entertainers: Madonna, Gwen Stefani, Christina Aguilera, Lady Gaga, Lindsay Lohan, Anna Nicole Smith, to name a few.

Marilyn Monroe demonstrated to her fans how she handled herself against the male-dominated Hollywood executives. Though she was always at the receiving end, Monroe never gave up. True fans understood what she was up against as she faced head-on the constant sexism from actors, directors, and other Hollywood executives.

Several brands continue to use her name, image, or likeness. Marilyn Monroe remains a true pop culture icon up to the twenty-first century.

Attention: Get Your Free Gift Now

Every purchase now comes with a FREE Bonus Gift

2020 Top 5 Fireside Books of the Year

(New-York Times Bestsellers, USA Today & more)

Get it now here:

Scan QR Code to Download Free Gift

Printed in Great Britain
by Amazon